Reflections of a Reformed

Control Freak ©

B.R. SMITH

Life Lessons I've
Learned Along The Way

"Reflections of a Reformed Control Freak – Life Lessons I've Learned Along The Way"

ISBN: 978-1-9742787-9-4

Published by Brinley Publishing,

Book printed by First Class Press

Book Interior and E-book Design by Amit Dey | amitdey2528@gmail.com

Key Words: Life Skills – Personal Development – Self Help

Front and Back Cover Design: Kimb Williams – kimbwilliams@shaw.ca

Front and Back Cover Photographs by Josh Jefferies – www.joshjefferies.com

Contact The Author: Brian Smith - brian@briansmithpld.com

Dedicated to Laura, my EA, CFO and LOML.
Thank you for your love and support and
for always believing in me.
You make all things possible

Life Lessons I've Learned Along The Way

Table of Contents

Introduction

Worth Remembering ...

"Your life is a planned event. Wishing and hoping won't make it so. When you change the habit – you change the result. But it won't change unless you do"

$\mathcal{M}$y first book *"Confessions of a Reformed Control Freak - The Top Ten Sins Most Managers Make & How to Avoid Them"* was written to guide managers and business leaders. It was suggested that the content would also benefit anyone needing or wanting to learn how to manage their time more effectively, cope with stress, and get along with just about anyone - even if you don't like them.

If you find yourself wanting more and are ready to make a change and live a more deliberate life, a life more for filling then this book is for you. It's filled with tips and techniques to help you make those kinds of changes.

Although I would like to tell you otherwise, it doesn't matter what book you read, the workshops you participated in or what seminar you will attend, even this book will **NOT** be the exception to the rule. There aren't any silver bullets here. Unless you apply the lessons in this book, your time and money will not be well spent.

Unless you are willing to make changes needed to live a more purposeful life – nothing will change. I'm here to help you succeed in any way I can. If you have questions looking for answers, please don't hesitate to reach out to me.

> *Unless you are willing to make changes needed to live a*
> *more purposeful life – nothing will change.*

I wish you all the best, Cheers

Worth Remembering ...

"The longer I live, the more I realize the impact of attitude on life. Attitude, to me, is more important than the past, than education, than money, than circumstances, than failures, than successes, than what other people think or say or do. It is more important than appearance, giftedness, or skill. It will make or break a company ... church ... a home. The remarkable thing is we have a choice every day regarding the attitude we will embrace for that day. We cannot change our past. We cannot change the fact that people will act in a certain way. We cannot change the inevitable. The only thing we can do is play on the one string we have, and that is our attitude. I am convinced that life is 10% what happens to me and 90% how I react to it. And so, it is with you. We are in charge of our attitudes.

*— **Charles Swindell***

A Word About Quotes

Quote – Verb. To speak of, write a passage from another, usually with credit/acknowledgment. To repeat a passage, borrow, quoting the motifs of past artists.

If you follow me on social media, you already know how much I love quotes. I use them all the time on my posts. You'll find some of my favourite quotes though out this book. I hope they'll inspire you as much as they have inspired me. I believe it's important to give credit where credit is due to the original author. If I didn't write it or don't know who did – the credit goes to Author Unknown. If you read one of the quotes and know who the original author is – please let me know.

Enduring Principals –
Your Personal Code of Conduct

*W*hat does it say about the world we live in when we question the honesty and integrity of the people in leadership positions – both in government and the clergy? Public trust in our lawyers, teachers, and financial institutions is at an all time low.

> **Worth Remembering ...** *"Leaders walk their talk; in true leaders there is no gap between the theories they espouse and their practice"* – **Warren Bennis**

What is ethical or unethical behaviour? Ethics is best described as a set of moral principles or values that defines what is considered right or wrong behaviour for a person or a group. Some people suggest that there is a difference between business ethics and personal ethics.

But, to my way of thinking, you are either ethical or you are not. There is only one kind of ethics. You either believe in being honest – to act with integrity – to be guided by a strong sense of values and fair play – or you do not. How can you behave one way at work and then behave differently at home and still be true to yourself – still be true to your code of conduct – your own set of enduring principles?

The first course I ever taught at Algonquin College's School of Business was a "Business Ethics" course developed by one of my heroes Professor Ron Knowles.

Professor Knowles developed the course for the first-year business students in our SME program (Small, Medium, Enterprises). One of the neat things about that course was I got to work with first-year business students to help them develop their code of conduct – their ethical decision-making model that they could use to help them make the right decision faced with an ethical dilemma. An ethical dilemma is when you are confronted with a situation where there is no clear right or wrong answer. There is no clear right or wrong way to behave.

> **Worth Remembering ...** *"Be more concerned with your character then your reputation. Your character is what you really are, while your reputation is what others think you are."*
> **– Dale Carnegie**

What do you hold to be true? What are your enduring principles? What are you not willing to compromise – no matter the situation – no matter the personal price you will have to pay? What series of questions do you ask yourself to solve your ethical dilemmas?

If you were to sit down and script your code of conduct, what kinds of things would you include? Do you believe in honesty? Do you believe in treating people fairly, consistently and with respect?

I have been put into positions in the past where I was forced to compromise my own set of values. I have done some things that I should have handled differently in hindsight because I ended up not being true to myself. What I did was not illegal, but it still bothers me to this day. I know it was the wrong thing to do. I should have acted differently, no matter the cost. When we behave in ways that conflict with our judgment of what is right, we lose faith in ourselves

You may not always make the right decision – regardless of what ethical decision-making model you use. But you can and will decide what you can live with no matter the outcome because you were true to yourself.

> **Worth Remembering ...** *"The depths and strength of a human character is defined by its moral reserves. People reveal themselves completely only when they are thrown out of customary conditions of their life, for only then do they have to fall back on their reserves." –* **Leon Trotsky**

The Josephson Institute of Ethics, a non-profit training and consulting organization based in Los Angeles, California, advocates moral decision-making based on six common values they call "The Six Pillars of Character".

The Institute contends that these six pillars are the basis of ethically defensible decisions and the foundation of well lived lives.

1. **Trustworthiness:** Honesty, integrity, reliability and loyalty
2. **Respect:** Civility, courtesy, tolerance and acceptance
3. **Responsibility:** Accountability, pursuit of excellence and self-restraint

4. Fairness: Process, impartiality and equity

5. Caring: Empathy, compassion and a sense of duty

6. Good Citizenship: A sense of fair play, giving back and giving a hand up.

What we say to ourselves and our actions must be congruent. Our words and our behaviour must match. There are people whom we trust and those we do not. And if we ask ourselves the reason why – most likely it is because we trust congruency and are suspicious of incongruence.

Results of a Society for Human Resources Management survey found that only 27% of the employees feel that their organization's leadership was ethical. You must be true to your personal code of conduct. If you must ask yourself if you acted ethically or not – you already know the answer.

Worth Remembering ...

"There is no reason not to follow your heart"

— Steve Jobs

Finding Your Why

The question to ask yourself is not what you do – the question to ask yourself is why you do it. Once you know your why all you need to do is find the courage to create your life around it. What really turns your crank? In a perfect world, what would you really love to be doing? What would it take for you to develop a career around it? What things need to fall into place for you to live a purposeful life – a life you envisioned for yourself ?

> ***Worth Remembering…*** *You were put on this earth to achieve your greatest self, to live out your purpose and do it courageously*
> **– Steve Maraboli**

Not sure what you were meant to be? What were you meant to do? For the next two weeks, I want you to write down what you were doing when you caught yourself smiling for no apparent reason. Every time you see yourself smiling or whistling or humming a song, write down what you were doing at that very moment. After your two weeks are up, look over your list. Do you see a pattern? You should be able to connect the dots and see the common denominator. It will reveal what you are truly meant to be doing. It will tell you what makes you happy.

> ***Worth Remembering …*** *The mystery of human existence lies in not just staying alive but in finding something to live for*
> **– Fyodor Dostoyevsky**

Once you have discovered what makes you happy, the next thing you need to figure out is how to make a living doing what you love to do. I genuinely love what I do. I cannot see myself doing anything else. You have within you the ability to do the same thing. You need to put a plan together to get there.

Caution: If you want to get into business for yourself, I do not recommend quitting your current job just yet. There are a lot of questions that need answers. Most new businesses fail within the first 3 to 5 years because of lack of funds or lack of management skills. Start slow; take baby steps. Operate it as a part-time business while you continue to work your full-time job. Do not be in a hurry to get there – you will get there soon enough.

How much income will your business need to generate before you can commit to it full time? How much income will it need to generate to be able to pay yourself a living wage? What are your monthly fixed costs? (Rent, hydro, phone, insurance, internet, etc.) What are your monthly revenue projections? Do the math. Live and die by the numbers. Revenue – Costs = Money left over to pay yourself and put back into the business so you can continue to grow. We tend to overestimate the amount of revenue coming in. I recommend that you have at least six months of savings in your bank account to cover all your expenses and pay yourself if your projections are wrong.

> ***Worth Remembering …*** *"You can't go back and change the beginning, but you can start where you are and change the ending." –* ***C. S. Lewis***

Finding your why is just the beginning. What you do with it is up to you. Do what you love to do and make a career out of it. I promise, you'll be glad you did.

Worth Remembering ...

"When you feel good, you open the door for positive energy to reach you."

– Unknown

Have You Ever Licked
a 9volt Battery?

*H*ave you ever licked a 9-volt battery? (I am not suggesting that you do – I am just asking if you have). When adults do something that makes them feel good, that gets them excited, what are they more apt to do? If you licked a 9-volt battery and liked that sensation, the more likely you would want to lick it again. I believe the key to motivating someone is to figure out what turns their crank. Figure out what they are looking to get out of the deal. People do things for their own reason – not yours. All you must do is figure out what is in it for them and use that to get them to do what you need to get done.

> **Worth Remembering** – *"It is only when a person has their own generator that we can talk about motivation. They need no outside stimulation."* – **Frederick Herzberg**

What motivates you to do what you do? I believe everyone can be motivated. I am sure of that. But not everyone is motivated by the same thing or in the same way. Some people are motivated by money. Some people are motivated by a fancy job title or that premier parking spot. You need to create an environment where people will want to motivate themselves.

Trust me, if you have the means to help them get what is in it for them, then you have their attention. If you do not, people will not be motivated enough to try.

Worth Remembering – *"Motivation Equation: Personal Want + Goal-Directed Behaviour = Your WIFFM – What is in It for Me"* – **Brian Smith**.

Motivation is inside out – never outside in. Most people are self-serving and will only do something if they get something out of the deal. Even someone who volunteers their time and energy is getting something from it, or they would not keep volunteering. The next time you need to motivate someone to do what you need to get done – instead of using the stick approach and hitting them over the head with it – try dangling a carrot. Trust me; it works every time. It is like licking a 9-volt battery.

Worth Remembering ...

"Coming together is a beginning. Keeping together is progress. Working together is success."

— Henry Ford

How to Get Along with People
Even if You Don't Like Them

*R*arely can you accomplish all that you set out to do without the help of someone else. You do not have to like the people you work with, but you need to learn how to get along with them. "Soft-Skills" or emotional intelligence as Daniel Goleman likes to refer them too – is a learned behavior.

> **Worth Remembering** ... *"Emotional intelligence - a common core of personal and social abilities has proven to be the key ingredient in people's success"*. – **Daniel Goleman**

A better understanding of yourself and understanding others' behaviours allows you to improve your performance in relationships, both at work and home. Your technical ability no longer guarantees success. Results of a study conducted by the Hay-Group, a leading authority on EQ (Emotional intelligence), show that EQ is twice as important for most jobs involving working with people; EQ is twice as important as IQ. (Sixty-seven percent of the competencies needed to work with others effectively are emotionally based).

Soft-skills is our ability to communicate and interact more effectively with others.

> **Worth Remembering** ... *"In organizations where people trust and believe in each other, they don't get into regulating and coercing behaviours. They don't need a policy for every mistake. People in these trusting environments respond with enormous commitment and creativity" –* **Walter Wriston**

Establishing a relationship built on mutual respect and trust is a process all humans must go through when they meet someone for the first time.

We take direction from and hang out with people we like. Trust and respect do not come automatically – you must earn both – one person at a time.

You must learn how to get along with people even if you do not like them. Success is a team sport. Just like it takes a village to raise a child – it takes a team to manage and lead an organization.

Think of someone you are having difficulty with. For whatever reason, you two are not getting along. It can be someone at work or in your social circles. I want you to take on this challenge and turn that situation around. I want you to apply a 3-step process known as the 3R's – I promise you will be amazed at how effective it is to establish those all-important relationships.

Step One: Rapport: Find out something about the other person other than the work they do. What are their hobbies? – Are they married? Do they have children? What do they like to do in their spare time? The easiest way to establish rapport with someone is to get them talking about themself. Ask questions, get interested in them, and then they will be interested in you.

Step Two: Relationship: You cannot have a relationship with anyone with whom you have not first established a rapport. The more that you can carry on a conversation with them on subjects that they are interested in – the more likely you are building a relationship with them. You are beginning to break down the barriers between you and the other person. You are starting to like each other.

Step Three: Respect: You will not respect anyone you have not developed a relationship with first. Respect is reciprocal. You must give it to get it. The more you treat someone the way you would like to be treated, the more likely they will respond in kind. You get back what you send out.

After respect comes trust. You never trust anyone you do not respect first. If you have established mutual respect in your relationship with the other person, they will trust you. They may not always agree with you – but they will respect the fact that you have an opinion and have a right to express it. So, go out and give it a try. You have nothing to lose – but a whole lot to gain.

Worth Remembering ...

"Whatever the circumstances of your life, the under-standing of type can make your perceptions clearer, your judgements sounder, and your life closer to your hearts desire."

—— **Isabel Briggs Myers**

If You Were a Tree What Kind of Tree Would You Be?

*I*f you were a tree, what kind of tree would you be? If you were a colour, do you think you would be red, blue, yellow, or green? What would you think if your interviewer asked you to draw a pig? Believe it or not, these are the kinds of questions you might get asked during your job interview. Do not panic; interviewers are not looking to have you committed. However, they are looking to gain valuable insight into your attitude, behaviour, and potential in the workplace.

Weird science? Perhaps. But today's behavioural assessment tools are becoming more and more prevalent as companies look for ways to hedge their bets against the high costs associated with hiring the wrong person.

Behavioural assessments are not new. Personality research dates back to Hippocrates in 400 BC. Hippocrates believed that we each have our own natural, perfect, unchangeable personality style. He believed that while we each have the same factors comprising our personalities, four distinct types of behaviour emerge.

It is interesting to note that no matter what assessment tool you use – Myers Briggs Type Indicator, Colours or DISC – they all agree that there are four distinct behaviour styles. Each style reacts to the same situation differently. And, we "fit" into one of the four types. Each of the four styles has its strengths and limitations; no one type is better than any other. However, some styles are better suited for some roles, tasks, or careers. Yes, we all indeed can modify our behaviour to get a different result, but we all have one style that feels most comfortable to us, and we use that one style most of the time, regardless of the circumstance. Keep in mind that a strength overused or used in the wrong situation can be a weakness.

Worth Remembering ... *"Effective executives fill positions and promote based on what a person can do. They do not make decisions to minimize weaknesses but to maximize strengths."* **– Peter F. Drucker**

Dr. William Marston first introduced DISC theory in his epic book, *Emotions of Normal People*, published in 1928. In the mid-1950s, William Clark further developed the Marston theory. He utilized the simple matrix entitled DISC and identified the factors that comprise each of the four styles. I believe the key to performance improvements is understanding ourselves better and studying others' behaviours.

Worth Remembering ... *"A common core of personal and social abilities has proven to be the key ingredient in people's success: emotional intelligence."* **– Daniel Goleman**

These are the four distinct styles of behaviour associated with DISC Theory. Recognize anyone you know? Which one sounds most like you?

D – Dominant Style, Direct and Decisive: These types of people make quick decisions when others cannot; they will confront challenging issues or situations, accept change as a personal challenge, keep the team focused on the task. In the past, we called this style the typical "A" Type personality. (I will let you figure out what the "A" meant.) Others might see limitations because they may come across as being unapproachable. They can be insensitive to others' needs. Patience is not a strong suit. D Style persons naturally want to take control. They have a lot of qualities that we like to see in our managers and leaders.

I – Interactive/Interpersonal Style, Optimistic and Outgoing: These people like to make themselves available to others; they spread their enthusiasm and positive attitude to others and give positive feedback to their colleagues and teammates. They are great communicators and have an innate ability to build collaborative teams. Others may see their limitations because they can appear to be disorganized. They love being around people, so they find it difficult to work alone. I Style people would rather be liked than respected. I Style persons make great salespeople – social convenors or teachers.

S – Steadiness Style, Sympathetic and Cooperative: These types are team players; they are sensitive to others' needs, approach meeting agendas methodically, and are great listeners. They are very loyal, show up to work on time, and maintain the status quo. They prefer to be non-confrontational. Others may see their limitations because they can be indecisive. They find it difficult to make quick decisions for fear of making waves and resist change for fear of failing. S Style persons work best in a structured environment where processes are defined, and they are expected to follow procedure.

C – Conscientious Style, Concerned and Correct: These types of people like things done the right way as they see it. They are very thorough and will maintain standards; (if they were the ones who developed the standard).

They emphasize accuracy and will try to use some diplomacy to get their way. C's are our very best planners. Others may see their limitations because they can be overly concerned with perfection. They prefer to work alone. C Style persons make great accountants, lawyers, or project managers.

Forget about spending your time improving upon your weaknesses. Learn to play to your strengths. We are all good at something. Embrace it, build a career around it and enjoy it.

Worth Remembering ...

"The more we believe we can control, the more we will try to control, and the more you will control."

—Author Unknown

If Your Life Sucks, It's Because You Do

*A*re you happy with what you are doing? If not, you need to take a good look in the mirror and realize that the only one getting in your way is you. You need to learn to get out of your way and live the life you intended. Don't let should have, could have or would have to be part of your vocabulary. What is getting in the way of you realizing your full potential and accomplishing your goals? Please take a moment and write down five things that are getting in your way to achieving your goals. You can't fix what you don't acknowledge.

> ***Worth Remembering ...*** *"You are the boss of you so act accordingly"* – ***Brian Smith***

You are the steward of your life, and you are responsible for your happiness. No one can make you choose the life you lead. It's a matter of choice – your choice. It is 100% in your control. You choose to be overweight. You choose to be poor. You choose to be miserable. You choose to blame others for your lot in life. When you get knocked down, you choose to stay down.

You have the power within you to make a change. You just need to decide what it is you'd like to change for the better. When you change the habit, you change the result. Can you create a new habit to get a different result? Replacing old habits with new ones is not easy, but you can do it.

Just stop doing one thing and start doing another – and if you do it often enough, it will become you. You have the capacity within you to make a change. You can learn to act in a way that is going to get you what you want.

Worth Remembering ... *"Good habits = good results. We are adults, and we can learn new habits."* **– Brian Smith**

It would be best if you decided when you've had enough of your old life. Until you get to that point, you won't be motivated enough to make a change. Motivation is inside out, never outside in.

If your life sucks, it's because you do. You suck at sticking to it and seeing it through. That's why most New Years resolutions fail because people give up too quickly. To make a change takes time. To make a change takes patience. To make a change, you must stop doing one thing and start doing another.

Change doesn't happen by chance. Change happens by following a process.

1. Decide what change or changes you want to make.
2. What do you have to stop doing?
3. What do you need to start doing - to make that change?
4. Start developing that new habit. Experts suggest you must do it 21 times in a row to establish a routine.
5. Keep doing it until you do it without thinking about it. Keep doing it until it becomes you.

The only thing getting in your way is you. You need to learn how to get out of your way.

Worth Remembering ...

"The greatest weapon we have against stress is our ability to choose one thought over another".

— ***William James***

Life Lessons: Learning to Cope with The "S" Word

The "S' word is all around us. It seems that we can- not go a day without hearing about it, feeling its effects, or getting caught up in it. It was not as topical 20 years ago, yet it has always been there. It just seems now it is on everyone's mind. The "S" word – yes, I am talking about STRESS! It is like that stone in your shoe that irritates the hell out of you until you remove it. You cannot eliminate all the stressors that are creating stress in your life, but you can learn how to deal with them.

Stress is not always a bad thing. A little bit of stress can be a very positive and motivating influence in our lives. Stress can help create a sense of urgency and force us to get off the couch.

Worth Remembering ... *"You must learn to let it go. Release the stress. You were never in total control anyway"* – **Steve Jobs**

When stress increases beyond our ability to cope with it easily, we begin to feel both its emotional and physical effects. (Headaches, inability to concentrate and a rise in our blood pressure) The adverse effects of everyday stressors are cumulative. A series of very mild stress events can create an exceptionally high-stress level if not dealt with effectively. You can learn how to cope.

Three Methods for Coping with Stress

Your most critical stress issues are those you feel are a high priority to change, and you can change them. Your least essential matters of stress are those with a low priority and are very difficult to change. Learn to change what you can, influence what you will and give up on those things you cannot control.

For those stressors you can change, the key is to develop a specific plan of action for creating the change you want and then follow through with that plan.

I know I make it sound simple, but it is that simple. For those stressors, you cannot change; the key is to change your response to them. If you cannot change them, you need to let them go because it wastes your t ime and energy.

Eliminate the stressors or change your response to them

To accomplish more with your life and achieve a more incredible feeling of satisfaction, you must reduce or eliminate unproductive stressors in your lives wherever and whenever possible. It will help if you improve your ability to cope with those stressors that you cannot stop. (You do not get to pick your relatives or immediate family, but you can choose how much time you spend with them)

Attitude – your attitude is 100% in your control. Only you get to decide how you want to react to any given set of circumstances. Only you get to choose when to take a few deep breaths to calm your- self, walk away or ignore it altogether.

Use the coping resources available to you

There are several social services available to you to help you cope with those significant life events like disease, divorce and even death. You do not have to carry the load yourself. Reach out. Reaching out is not a sign of weakness. Reaching out is a sign of strength.

Hobbies are also a great way to de-stress at the end of the day. Exercising, eating right, and getting enough sleep will also help reduce the ill effect of stress in your life.

Develop new coping resources

You only know what you only know. If what you are currently doing to cope is not working, you need to discover a better way. Read a book, attend a workshop, or better yet, join a support group.

> **Worth Remembering ...** *"If you want to conquer the anxiety of life, live in the moment, live in the breath."* **—Amit Ray**

The last thing you should do is sit at home alone with too much time on your hands. The last thing you should do is sit alone at home feeling sorry for yourself. Getting knocked down is not the issue. Every- one gets knocked down. Not getting back up and doing something about it is the issue. You can learn to deal with the "S" word. It is 100% in your control.

Worth Remembering ...

"Failure is not the opposite of success – failure is part of it."

– Unknown

Success Comes by Learning to Fail Magnificently

$\mathcal{J}$f you are going to fail – you might as well fail magnificently. And if you aren't failing, chances are you aren't trying hard enough. If you aren't failing, you are going through life, playing it way too safe. You are robbing yourself of your opportunity to grow.

I don't think we start out intentionally to fail – but we shouldn't let the fear of failing get in the way of giving it a go. Failing is part of the learning process. It's a way of figuring out what works – and more importantly – what doesn't work.

Worth Remembering ... *"I have not failed 10,000 times – I have discovered 10,000 ways that do not work" – Thomas Edison.*

Imagine what life would have been like in Edison's time if he had given up. I know for sure that he would never have realized his full potential if he had given up. Where would Michael Jordan be today if he had given up on basketball after being cut from his high school basketball team? Like Michael Jordan, I've been knocked down so many times I've lost count.

Getting knocked down has never been an issue for me. If I want it bad enough, I will get back up, dust myself off and press on. Hopefully, a little wiser and a little more informed.

How bad do you want it? Are you willing to get knocked down? Are you ready to look for the lessons and learn from them? Are you willing to get back up and press on? The word quitter should not be part of your vocabulary.

Don't rob yourself of your opportunity to grow. Personal growth happens outside of your comfort zone.

What do you want? What must happen for you to reach your goal? Success comes by learning to fail magnificently. Now put a game plan together and get busy.

Worth Remembering …

"Where your attention goes, your time goes".

— Idowu Koyenikan

The Key to Time Management
is Life Management

*W*e all face the daily dilemma of having too much to do and not enough time to do it. The problem isn't that you have too much to do – the problem is you are trying to do too much. We have 168 hours over the course of a week – no more – no less. Time in not adaptable – people are. Time isn't out of control – we are.

The secret to good time management is good self-management. The secret to good self-management is good habits. We are adults, and we can develop new habits. You have to stop doing one thing and start doing another. And the more that you do it, the more it becomes you.

Worth Remembering ... *"Besides the noble art of getting things done, there is the noble art of leaving things undone. The wisdom of life consists of eliminating the non-essentials"* **– Chinese Proverb.**

Your Daily To-Do List

- Determine your daily, weekly, and monthly goals. What do you want to accomplish? Write them down on your To-Do List.

- Read your list at least three times a day. In the morning - after lunch – and at the end of your day just before you nod off to sleep. You need to wake up in the morning with a sense of urgency. It would be best if you got up in the morning and hit the ground running.

- Don't try to keep your goals in your head. Writing them down helps to de-clutter your brain. If you've written it down, you won't forget it. By writing it down, you've made a personal contract with yourself. You've made a personal commitment to accomplish that goal. I always feel a great sense of accomplishment when I stroke an item off my To-Do List after completing it.

Establishing Priorities:

Think carefully about what priorities mean to you and about how you decide what is essential. Remember – you will never have enough time over your day, week, or month to accomplish everything on your To-Do List. But you do have the time to decide what needs to be completed today.

Know Your A, B, C's

Try this simple but effective A-B-C System to help you decide when to do what on your list.

- An **"A"** item is an urgent item, and it needs your immediate attention because it must be accomplished today.
- Anything that needs to be completed in 2 or 3 days should be labelled a **"B'** item.
- Anything else on your list should be labelled a **"C"** item.

Never, never, ever work on a **"B"** item until all of your **"A"** items have been completed for that day. If all your **"A"** items have been completed, you can start working on a **"B"** item. You can use systems to help you prioritize what needs to be done and when. The key is being disciplined enough to stick to your plan.

Learn to Play The What If Game

Learn to play the what-if game to help you decide which **"A"** item you will to start working on first. Look at all the **"A"** items on your list and ask yourself, if I don't do this one – what's the worst thing that can happen? Don't start on the easy ones. Start on the ones that will affect you the most. How you manage your time is how you manage your life.

> **Worth Remembering ...** *"Time management is really a misnomer. The challenge we face is not to manage time, but to manage ourselves." –* **Stephen Covey**

Are You Using Your Time Wisely?

Grab a pen and paper and try this little exercise. Take a moment and think about the three most important things in your life.

They can be friends, family, career, etc. Now write those three things down on that paper. How much of your time do you spend on the top 3 things you put on your list? Did you put yourself at the top of that list? We seldom do.

You have limited time and energy after the time you spend at work, sleeping, meals, personal hygiene and other commitments.

Make sure you're spending some of your 168 on those three things that are most important to you.

Eventually, we all run out of time. If you want to avoid the time crunch, make sure you schedule some of your time each week on what you value the most. Even an hour a week is better than nothing. Most people regret that they didn't spend enough time on what brought them joy and contentment on their death bed.

Worth Remembering ….

"It is not enough to be busy. The question is, what are we busy about?"

— Henry David Thoreau

Think it – Act it – Become it – Developing Self Confidence

*W*hat is your biggest obstacle to more self-confidence? I think it is your internal dialogue – the way you talk to yourself. If you think negative thoughts – then negative things will happen. It is the law of attraction happening in real-time. A low self-image translates into a lack of confidence – which causes us to think negative thoughts, which causes us to hold back and give up easily rather than face tough challenges.

Worth Remembering ... *"Lack of confidence is not the result of difficulty. The difficulty comes from the lack of confidence".* – **Seneca**

"The better people think they are, the better they will be. A positive self-image creates success' – Lisa Joronen. World-class athletes, like world-class actors, visualize a Gold Medal – Oscar-winning performance. They set themselves up for a positive experience by visualizing in their mind's eye what their performance will look like, and then they go out and replay that winning performance in real-time.

You need to visualize your gold medal-winning performance and then play that video for real. The more you do it – the more you will become it.

Five Ways to Develop Self Confidence:

- **Look for a role model or mentor.** What is it about their style that you like? What do they do that makes them appear confident? (Their walk, the way they look or the way they talk?) Act as they act, and you will eventually begin to perform the same way. I love Tom Peter's style when he delivers a speech (Author of "In Search of Excellence") When I first began giving speeches, I emulated his style, and eventually, it became my style. I created a "Habit" and I now do it without thinking about it. A good habit is a good result – plain and simple.

- **Focus on your achievements rather than your failures.** Focus on what you did well and what you will do better the next time you have the same opportunity. We can all improve. We have all done things that, in hindsight, we would have done differently. I am forever critiquing myself, but it is the only way I know how to get better at what I do. How often have you had an exchange with someone that turned ugly? And after you calmed down, you went over it again in your mind and realized that you could have handled it better? Remember – Nobody is perfect, but everyone can grow and get better.

- **Set reachable goals for yourself.** Set SMART targets. Break down difficult tasks into more bite-sized pieces. Anyone can eat an elephant one bite at a time. I love the feeling I get when I cross an item off on my To-Do list. It is even better when I have completed everything on the page, and I get to tear it out of my notebook and throw that page away.

- **Be prepared for every task.** Nothing beats thinking and planning it out. You cannot be prepared for everything, but you should be able to predict the kinds of things that could happen and how you react to them.

You should anticipate the kinds of questions you will be asked and script your answers in advance. If you have are well prepared, you will look confident, and the other person will think you are. Communication is 93% non-verbal. It is not what you say that people remember – it is how you went about saying it that people remember the most.

Remember to be your authentic self. You are not in competition with anyone but yourself. You are unique. You are who you are. You can only do what you can do. Strive to be the very best that you can be. Feel good about yourself knowing that you gave 100% of your- self. You cannot do better than that.

> ***Worth Remembering …*** *"Do or do not. There is no try"* **– Yoda.**

Someone who is confident in their abilities and is comfortable in their skin will not need to hold anyone else down to feel better about themselves. What do you want people to think and say about you? Think it, act it, become it. Be that person.

Worth Remembering ...

"The harder you fall, the heavier your heart; the heavier your heart; the stronger you climb; the stronger you climb, the higher your pedestal".

— **Author Unknown**

You Are Producing
a Generation of Wimps

Stop the madness!!! You are producing a generation of wimps. As a parent or coach, your job is to teach life skills and not be someone's best friend. In the "real" world, not everyone gets to make the team, regardless of their skill level. In the "real" world, they won't be praised or promoted for just showing up. And in the "real" world, they may not get a second chance to make the wrong thing right, without paying the price for being wrong in the first place.

In the "real" world there are consequences. You are doing this newest generation a disservice by not preparing them for life "outside" of the nest. The world can be a cruel place for someone who hasn't been taught the skills needed to take on life's challenges. The world can be a cruel place for someone who hasn't been knocked down because they never learn how to get back up. The world can be a cruel place for someone who rarely heard the word "NO" while growing up.

Tough love applied at the right time – for the right reasons – is not a bad thing. Tough love teaches you that life is not always fair. You don't get everything that you ask for. You don't always make the team. Tough love teaches you that bad things can happen to good people. Tough love teaches you to stand up on your own two feet and compete for what you want. Tough love builds character, self-confidence, and self-esteem.

> **Worth Remembering ...** *"There is nothing more unequal than the equal treatment of unequal people."*
> **– Thomas Jefferson**

When you eliminate honour rolls or dean lists in schools because you don't want to make those who want to skate by not feel inferior – you take away the incentive for the achievers who want to excel.

You can't build up someone's self-worth by taking away someone else's.

When you no longer keep score because you don't want the other team to "feel" discouraged, you take away a person's competitive spirit. If you don't teach them the value of money, you take away what it means to be independent and the feeling they'll get from making it on their own – you are robbing them of their opportunity to grow.

> **Worth Remembering ....** *"Suck it up buttercup. Life isn't fair. Life is what you make it".* **- Author Unknown**

You can be someone's soft place to fall, but you must let them fall before you pick them up. Failure is a good thing. If you want to stop producing a generation of wimps, then let them fail.

Worth Remembering ...

"If you don't know where you are going, you might wind up someplace else. By failing to prepare, you are preparing to fail. Our goals can only be reached through a vehicle of a plan, in which we must fervently believe, and upon which we must vigorously act. There is no other route to success".

— Author Unknown

We Are All Just Passing Through

*A*s I approach my 70th birthday, I am reminded that I have more years behind me than what lies ahead of me. Time, unfortunately, is not a renewable resource. We all have just 168 hours in a week, approximately 672 in a month and 8,064 in a year. No more or no less. Are you spending your time wisely? If someone told you that you had just one more year to live – what is the one thing on your to-do list that you would want to accomplish? What is that one thing that you have always wanted to do but kept putting it off, thinking that you had all kinds of time? Name one thing.

Worth Remembering ... *"A lot of us think we are invincible .... but we have to start putting ourselves on the to-do list". – Unknown*

Take a moment and write down that one pressing thing you would like to accomplish. Would you like to go on a world cruise, learn to play guitar, write a book, or skydive? Make it a BIG one. No sense thinking small here. Remember, you only have a year.

My Dad retired at an early age. Before he passed away some 30 years later at the age of 85, he had taken up golf, tried his hand at needlepoint and crochet, joined Facebook so he could keep up to date with what was happening with family and friends and joined several service clubs. My Dad managed to tick a lot of things off his to-do list. How are you doing with yours?

Write the one thing that you would like to accomplish here:

I would like to accomplish:

_____

_____

_____

_____

_____

_____

_____

What is it going to take for you to accomplish that goal? I want you to write those things down as well. Once you have written all of them down, I want you to put a plan together to accomplish each one. Anyone can eat an elephant one bite at a time. Keep your eye on the prize and work on your plan.

For me to accomplish my goal I must:

- _____

- _____

- _____

- _____

Worth Remembering ... *"Those who every morning plans the transactions of that day and follows that plan, carries a thread that will guide them through the labyrinth of the busiest life."*
— *Victor Hugo*

As you start to work on your plan, please think of these three things.

1. Only do those things that move you forward. If it does not move you closer to accomplishing your goal, you need to be disciplined enough to say no. If it does not move you closer to achieving your goal, then you are wasting valuable time. The time that you cannot afford to give up. It would be best if you manage your time well.

2. You need to eliminate all the distractions in your life. You need to walk away from those who are robbing you of your time. That includes family, friends, and acquaintances. You know who the time wasters are. You need to be selfish here. Now do not get me wrong, all work and no play makes for a dull life. Life is a journey that should be enjoyed. So, when it is time to work — work. And when it is time to play — play a little — and then get back to work.

3. Focus, focus, focus. Time is not a renewable resource. Never take your eyes off the prize. Remember, we are all just passing through.

Worth Remembering ...

"There is no such thing as a bad listener. There is only a person with inflexible listening habits."

—Doug Larson

Why People Tune-Out &
What You Can Do About It

We are not wired to be good listeners, but we can learn to be. Research conducted by Dr. Ralph Nichols, a founding member of the International Listening Association, revealed that individuals listen about 25% of the time, most people only recall 50% of what they hear, and 70% of all misunderstandings happen because people do not listen to each other.

Worth Remembering ... *"I listen to understand, not necessarily to agree."* – **Carnegie**

That same survey revealed that grade school children listen to their teachers, just 25% of the time. By the time young people graduate from high school, they are listening to the teacher only 17% of the time, and by the time they graduate college, they are listening to the professor just 12% of the time. Based on those percentages, is it any wonder that you feel no one is listening to you.

Have you ever observed two people having a conversation and knew that neither one was not listening? They were just waiting for the other person to catch their breath and stop talking so they could jump in and take over the conversation. Two monologues do not make a dialogue.

Worth Remembering ... *"We have two ears but only one mouth. Some people suggest that is because we should spend twice as much time listening than talking. Others suggest it's because listening is twice as hard." –* ***Dr. Ralph Nichols***

We all suffer from natural tune-out. It is no wonder because we listen and speak at two different rates of speed. The average person can speak at a rate of 125 to 150 words per minute. Yet, your mind can comprehend and process information at an average rate of 500 words per minute. If you do the math that it adds up to a gap of some 350 words.

Develop Good Listening Habits

We are adults, and we can learn new habits. Stop doing one thing and start doing another, and if you do it often enough, you will have developed a new habit. Experts suggest if you do the new routine 21 times in a row, it will become you.

- **Patience:** Be patient with yourself and the speaker. Concentrate on what the speaker is saying. Do not interrupt. When they have finished talking, ask them some questions, so you know what was said. It also sends a powerful message to the speaker that you were listening.

- **Focus:** Focus on the speaker so you can hear what they are saying. Smile, face the speaker, do not look at your cell phone, put down whatever is in your hands and give the speaker your undivided attention.

- **Open-Mindedness:** Do not become emotional. React and respond to what is being said, not to who is saying it.

Respect the fact that people have a right to express their opinion. You can agree to disagree.

Worth Remembering ... *The most basic of all human needs is the need to understand and be understood."* – *Dr. Ralph Nichols.*

Active Listening Skills

The act of hearing is defined as being able to perceive someone's sound or something with the ear. Staying in the moment and actively listening and hearing what is being said can be difficult.

To listen requires mental and verbal paraphrasing and attention to non-verbal cues like tone of voice, gestures, and facial expressions. The next time you have an opportunity to listen to someone, try to be actively involved.

Develop and demonstrate these five skills to become a better listener.

1. **Restating and Summarizing:** You should restate what the other person said and or summarize the discussion. The speaker should hear their own words played back to them. (So, if I heard you correctly, you said ....)

2. **Paraphrasing:** It goes beyond restating and summarizing because you give them your interpretation of what you heard them say.

3. **Non-Words:** You can show the speaker that you are actively listening by using what I call green light responses. (ah …huh, yeah, hmmm, oh, etc.)

4. **Supporting Statements:** Another way to acknowledge the speaker is to use supporting statements like verbally; Go on, tell me more – and then what happened? – I see what you mean.

5. **Non-Verbal Messages:** We communicate 55% of the time by body language alone. You are speaking volumes, and you have not said a word. What you are saying and the non-verbal messages your body is sending must be congruent.

Arms crossed and looking around the room tells the speaker that you are not interested in them or what they are saying.

Remember – People tune out because they sense you haven't tuned in.

Worth Remembering ...

"A skeptic is someone who keeps an open mind but requires vigorous investigation before choosing to believe something."

– Thomas E. Kida

Don't Believe Everything
You See and Think

*H*ave you ever met someone for the very first time and thought "what a dink"? And I do not mean Double Income No Kids. There was just something about them that you did not like. I thought that when I first met Morris – Laura's cat. As a kid growing up, I never hung around with cats. We were dog people; all my friends were dog people, so I never had much use for cats.

We all have built-in biases based on our own experiences. We are influenced by what we read, hear, and see, so it is no wonder I never got to know cats.

After taking the time to get to know someone, have you ever changed your opinion about them? Meeting and getting to know Morris helped me change my opinion about cats.

> ***Worth Remembering...*** *There are things known and there are things unknown. And in between are the doors of perception.* – *Aldous Huxley*.

Perception: a way of regarding, understanding, or interpreting something, a mental impression that is rarely based on facts. Your perception is your reality. It is whatever you think it is.

However, we know that first impressions can be wrong. Do not believe everything you see and think. Do not let your preconceived notions get in the way of the decisions you make.

As a college professor, I encouraged my business students always to question the status quo. To continue to seek out others who have a different point of view. To ask open-ended questions and really listen to the answers and always make sure you have all the facts before you decide anything. Have you ever made a decision that ended up being the wrong one after you got all the facts? I know I have.

Worth Remembering ... *One of the biggest problems with the world today is that we have large groups of people who will accept whatever they hear on the grapevine just because it suits their worldview – not because it is actually true or because they have evidence to support it. – Neil deGrasse Tyson*

Intuition – instinct, insight, sixth sense, discernment, call it what you will. But verify before you act, assume nothing or it may come back and bite you.

I watched the movie "The Shape of Water" which reminded me never to believe everything you see and think.

Worth Remembering ...

"There is nothing more annoying than somebody who is really thick but who believes with absolute conviction that they are more intelligent than you."

— **Karl Wiggins**

Maybe It is Time to Thin the Herd

Forest Gump said it best – "Stupid is what stupid does." Some say you can't fix stupid. If that is the case, then maybe it is time to thin the herd. There might be something to be said for Darwin's theory, the survival of the fittest.

Now I'm not advocating that we start rounding people up, but you must admit that some people say and do the dumbest things. Their elevator isn't going all the way to the top. If we were counting bricks, they would be a few bricks short of a load. I'm not talking about those that have a medical condition or are mentally challenged. I'm talking about people who are smart enough to know better. It's time people started to think, or put on a dunce cap and sit in the corner!!! For most of us, being stupid is a choice – so stop playing dumb.

> **Worth Remembering ...** *"Only two things are infinite, the universe and human stupidity, and I'm not sure of the former."*
> **- .Mark Twain**

Here is a partial list of my pet peeves. They appear here in no particular order. Feel free to add yours to this list.

1 – People that state the obvious. (Excuse me, do you work here?) I guess wearing a company uniform wasn't a big enough clue for them.

2 – People who walk into a store and stop at the front entrance to have a conversation or look around are blocking everyone else from getting in or getting out.

3 – People who fail to maintain the passing lane's speed limit are oblivious to the miles of traffic behind them.

4 – Truck drivers passing other trucks on the highway. One driver is doing 60 – trying to pass a truck that's doing 59 miles an hour.

5 – People who wait until the cashier has rung in all their purchases and bagged the items before they start looking for the money to pay for them.

6 – People who hold up the line looking for exact change to pay for their purchase – usually all in coins.

7 – Salespeople who say "no problem" instead of "my pleasure" when I thank them for helping me. I know it's not a problem – that's why you're there.

8 – People who haven't figured out yet why popular fast-food restaurants post their menu on the wall over top of the order taker. They wait until their turn to order before looking over the menu board and deciding what they want.

9 – People who ask a question and then appear not to be interested in the answer. They seem to be paying attention to everyone else in the room, but you.

10 – People who bring a cell phone onto the golf course and hold everyone else up while they take a call. (It usually rings in the middle of your backswing)

11 – People who carry on a cell phone conversation loud enough so everyone in the restaurant can hear.

12 – People who have not figured out yet what turn signals are for, or they know but decide not to use them.

Worth Remembering ... *"I'm the only person who says don't force the stupid people to be quiet. I want to know who the morons are." – Author Unknown*

Ignorance is a choice. People choose to be stupid. They choose to be stupid because they refuse to do some fact-checking and learn something new. Common sense is a myth. There isn't any. They should call it life sense.

Hopefully, the older we get, the smarter we get. I know for some that is a bit of a stretch. Maybe it's time to thin the herd.

Worth Remembering ...

We are being judged by a new yardstick: not just how smart we are, or by our training and expertise, but also by how well we handle ourselves and each other. – **Daniel Goleman**

Why Women Should Rule The World

*W*hy Women make better leaders can be summed up in just one word – "Empathy". Empathy, the ability to be able to see a situation from another person's point of view. Emotion researchers generally define empathy as the ability to sense others people's emotions, coupled with the ability to imagine what someone else might be thinking or feeling. Women seem to come by it natu rally, while most men must work at developing it.

If there ever was a time for authentic leadership, it's now. Dee Dee Myers, author of *"Why Women Should Rule The World"* believes that women are more successful in running businesses because women can make people accountable for their actions but are also there to support them. Women around the world are rewriting history. It's easy to argue that men haven't been doing such a great job lately. That's not meant to be a political statement; I'm just stating the facts. Anna Crowe, CEO and Founder of Crowe PR, believes that most women have a strong understanding of what drives and motivates people to perform at their personal best and how to acknowledge different people for their performance.

Worth Remembering *... "Many women, especially moms, are trained caretakers and know how to deal with crisis situations at home with compassion and patience. These* *attributes become very relevant when a women leader is dealing with crises situations whether this is related to HR or Clients." – **Huma Gruaz***

Do you have what it takes to be a world-class leader?

- **True leaders** understand themselves and how their attitude affects others.

- **True leaders** understand that they must communicate in a way that others will understand.

- **True leaders** understand that every situation is different, so they know they must behave and respond differently. One leadership style does not fit all.

- **True leaders** realize that they need their people more than their people need them. They understand that success is a team effort.

- **True leaders** know they don't have to have all the answers, so they need to surround themselves with people who do.

- **True leaders,** above all, understand that they must lead by example.

- **True Leaders** park their ego at the door, do what they need to do to complete the task, and to reach the goal.

- **True leaders** understand that it doesn't have to be just their way.

Worth Remembering ... *"Women make great leaders because we are flexible and agile. We can see the direction we thought we should take, and we regroup and change course for the better."*
*– **Danita Harris***

I could go on, but I think you get my point. Women deserve far more credit than they have been given. Gender shouldn't be a factor in whether a person has what it takes to be a true leader.

True leaders must master the ability to connect with others and build collaborative teams.

True leaders must master the ability to communicate in a way that others will understand. True leaders must master the ability to teach others what they need to know and delegate successfully.

If you're looking to develop 21st Century leadership skills, then take a page out of their play book. You'll be better for it, and so will the people you lead.

Worth Remembering ...

"Have no fear of perfection – you'll never reach it."

– Salvador Dali

In Most Cases Perfection is Highly Overrated

Sorry if I am the one to burst your bubble, but nobody is Sperfect. Not even you. You do not need to handicap yourself by carrying around that kind of burden. Aim for the bulls-eye. Strive for perfection - yes, but understand that sometimes you cannot attain the unattainable. Sometimes you are going to fall short and miss the target. Do not beat yourself up over it. You can take pride in the fact that you did your very best. You gave it your all. And if you truly gave it your all, then you have no more to give. You can only give 100%. Learn to accept that what it is, shortcomings and all. Eliminate the stressors in your life, chances are you will live longer.

Worth Remembering ... *"An environment that calls for perfection is not likely to be easy. But aiming for it is always good progress." –* ***Thomas Watson Jr.***

According to most psychologists' people move in a direction that is opposite to the direction they want to avoid. In other words, perfectionists strive for perfection because they do not feel that they are perfect. Because they somehow feel inferior to other people in certain situations and try to overcome their perceived shortcomings. In the long run, striving for perfection can destroy your self-confidence.

Worth Remembering ... *"Perfection is not attainable, but if we chase perfection, we can catch excellence."* **Vince Lombardi**

Paralysis by analysis. Overthinking can be a deal-breaker. There is no such thing as the perfect plan. You cannot think of everything that could or would go wrong. If you wait for perfection before executing your plan, when early action would have been preferable, you stand the chance of missing your opportunity for success. Sometimes good enough is good enough. In most cases, perfection is highly overrated.

Worth Remembering ...

"When you allow your ego to control your thoughts, everything you believe becomes an illusion.

– Rusty Eric

Sometimes It's Best to Park Your Ego at The Door

*Y*ou and I both know there are several ways to accomplish the same thing. Does it have to be your way? You're in charge. You're going to get the credit. However, the more you allow others to be involved in the process, the more likely they will be interested in the results. Don't let your ego get in the way of doing the kinds of things you need to do to get others to buy into what you want to get done.

> ***Worth Remembering …*** *"Drop the idea that you are Atlas carrying the world on your shoulders. The world would go on even without you. Don't take yourself too seriously."*
> **– Norman Vincent Peale**

Now don't get me wrong. It's important to have a healthy ego. Trust me. I have enough ego to fill up any room I walk into. My ego has never been in short supply. But remember that a strength overused or used in the wrong situation can become a weakness. It's like stress. A little stress in your life is not necessarily a bad thing. Without a bit of stress in our lives, we'd turn into couch potatoes and would never get motivated enough to want to do anything.

Worth Remembering … *"Bury your ego. Don't be the star. Be the star-maker." –* ***Bud Hadfield***

A little ego gives us enough self-confidence in our abilities to step up and take on specific tasks or play a particular role. If you have too much ego, you may volunteer to take something on but then have too much pride to admit you're in over your head and ask for help if things go wrong. Asking for help is not a sign of weakness. Having some humility and admitting you made a mistake is a sign of strength. Sometimes it's best to park your ego at the door.

Worth Remembering ...

"A positive attitude gives you power over your circumstances instead of your circumstances having power over you."

– Unknown

Is Your Cup Half Full or Half Empty?

"For myself – I am an optimist. It does not seem to be much use being anything else". Churchill was right. Do you walk around thinking that your cup is half-full or half-empty? I choose to see my cup as half-full. I choose to see the positives in everything that happens to me because everything that happens to me is an opportunity to learn.

Even the negative things that happen to you, and trust me, there will be plenty of positive ones if you learn to look at them from a different perspective.

> **Worth Remembering ...** *"The bend in the road is not the end of the road unless you fail to make the turn." – **Amanda Curtis Kane***

Attitude – your attitude is a matter of choice. You own it 100% of the time. Only you get to decide how you want to react to any given situation. You are the boss of you. You can choose to look at the negative things that will happen to you and wallow deep down in the muck, or you can choose to learn from them and grow. You can choose to learn the lessons the negatives are trying to teach you and move forward. You always have a choice.

***Worth Remembering* ...** *"Between stimulus and response there is a space. And in that space lies our freedom and power to choose our response. In those choices, lies our growth and happiness."*
– Stephen R. Covey

Viktor Frankl understood the power to choose. Viktor understood that no one else but he could decide how he should react to any given situation. Viktor was an Austrian-born Neurologist and Psychiatrist best known for founding Logotherapy, a theory used when working with people contemplating suicide.

During WWII, the Nazi's had taken away all that was dear to him. He lost his precious manuscripts, his loving parents, and siblings. Viktor had a choice to make. He knew he had no control over what they had done to him and his family, but he could control how he chooses to react to it. Like Viktor, we all have a choice. We can choose to find the positives in the negatives.

***Worth Remembering* ...** *"When defeat comes, accept it as a signal that your plans are not sound. Rebuild those plans and set sail once more towards your goal." – Napoleon Hill*

Having a relationship with my son was and still is very important to me.

But to have a relationship with my son, I needed to have a relationship with his mother, my soon to be ex-wife. I had a choice to make. I could choose to be confrontational and drag out the divorce proceedings, or I could choose to negotiate a settlement that we both could agree with. I decided to negotiate a fair settlement. I decided to see the positives in a negative situation.

> **Worth Remembering ...** *"Attitude is a choice. Happiness is a choice. Optimism is a choice. Kindness is a choice. Giving is a choice. Respect is a choice. Whatever choice you make makes you. Choose wisely.* **– Bennett**

Is your cup half-full or half-empty?

Worth Remembering …

"If you are lucky enough to get a second chance, don't waste it."

– Unknown

Worth Remembering …

"When people are ready to, they change. They never do it before then, and sometimes they die before they get around to it. You can't make them change if they don't want to, just like when they do want to change, you can't stop them."

– Andy Warhol

Stop Trying to Change People

*E*verybody is good at something. Some people are good planners while others are better at executing those plans. Not everyone can sing a song well, but they can play an instrument.

We have listened to great communicators and some who have a difficult time being understood. It is very rare to find someone who is good at everything.

> ***Worth Remembering*** *... "Consider how hard it is to change yourself, and you will begin to understand what little chance you have in trying to change others." –* ***Unknown***

You cannot take the stripes off a tiger or rub the spots off a leopard no matter how hard you try. Stop wasting your time by trying to change people. You cannot. You would have more luck trying to herd cats. Trust me – that is darn near impossible.

Think like a leader and put people in positions where they can do what they do well.

> ***Worth Remembering*** *... "The task of an executive is not to change human beings. The task is to multiply the performance capacity of the whole by putting to use whatever strength, whatever health, whatever aspiration there is in individuals."* *–* ***Peter F. Drucker***

I have learned by trial and error and mostly error to do what I do well and leave everything that I do not do well to others. I know nothing about repairing a vehicle, even though I managed a very successful and profitable vehicle repair service department. I left the vehicles' repairing up to the automotive technicians while I balanced the books and cared for the customers.

Worth Remembering ...

"Trust is the glue of life. It is the most essential ingredient in effective communication. It is the foundational principle that holds relationships together.

– Unknown

Trust is a Two-Way Street

Sometimes you need others to take a leap of faith. Without first establishing trust, you will have little chance of getting people to come along. If they trust you, they will follow you. If they trust you, they will believe you have their best interest in mind. If they trust you, they will think that you are not setting them up to fail.

> **Worth Remembering ...** *"It takes 20 years to build a relationship and five minutes to ruin it."* – **Warren Buffet**

Are you looking to establish trust? Start here

Keep Your Word. Your word is your bond. Whatever you say you are going to do – do it. If they cannot trust what you say – they will not trust you.

Be Honest and Transparent. Tell the truth – always. If people catch you in a lie, you will never regain their trust.

Admit You Do Not Have All the Answers. It is ok if you do not have all the answers. However, you need to know who and where to go to get them.

Admit When You've Made a Mistake. We all make mistakes. It is part of the learning process. Take ownership, learn from them, apologize, and move on.

Be True to Your Own Set of Values. Do not compromise your own set of values. Do not sell your soul to the highest bidder. Be true to who you are. Integrity is more than just a word. Maintaining your integrity should not be for sale.

> ***Worth Remembering*** ... *A single lie discovered is enough to create doubt in every truth expressed.* – ***Unknown***

Trust is a two-way street.

Worth Remembering …

"Patience is the calm acceptance that things can happen in a different order than the one that you have in mind."

— David G. Allen

Learn to Count to Ten

*A*ccording to Wikipedia, patience is defined as the ability to endure difficult circumstances such as perseverance in the face of delay, tolerance of provocation without responding in anger, or forbearance when under strain, especially when faced with longer-term difficulties. In today's turbulent times, we could all use a little more patience. Picking up a baseball bat and smacking someone on the side of the head because you are frustrated might not be the best way to go. You need to learn to count to ten.

> ***Worth Remembering*** *...* *"Patience is bitter, but it's fruit is sweet." –* ***Aristotle***

Are you looking to develop more patience? Here are some things to keep in mind.

1. **Expect challenges.** There is no such thing as a perfect plan. Something will go wrong, and when it does, work around it or climb over it.

2. **Go slow to go fast.** You do not want to end up doing things twice. Get all the facts before deciding but decide in a timely manner. Procrastination is a killer.

3. **Be empathetic.** People will make mistakes; everyone does. When mistakes happen, fix them, do not dwell on them, and not remind them that they made a mistake.

4. **See the BIG picture.** Do not get bogged down in the weeds. A minor setback is just that. Take a deep breath and keep moving forward.

5. **What is your WIIFM?** If you can learn to develop patience, what is in it for you? What will developing patience do for you? Will it help you cope with the stressors in your life? Will it help reduce tension and anxiety? Will it improve relationships both at work and at home?

Worth Remembering ... *"He that can have patience can have what he will." –* ***Ben Franklin***

Those that know me best know that patience has never been my strong suit. It is something I have had to work at. Those that know me best know that I am still a work in progress. I have had to bite my tongue on more than one occasion. I have had to learn to count to ten.

Worth Remembering ...

"The difference between great people and everyone else is that great people create their lives actively, while everyone else is created by their lives, passively while waiting to see next where life takes them. The difference between the two is the difference between living fully and just existing."

– Michael E. Gerber

Three Must Have Leadership Skills

 $\mathscr{J}$ f you do a Google search for the top ten traits of great leaders, more than likely you will find having the ability to make quality decisions, able to pass work on to others and being exceptional communicators are on that list. Managing and leading others is a learned behaviour. Suppose you have aspirations of managing or taking on a leadership position in your organization. In that case, I believe you need to learn how to communicate and interact more effectively, learn to make decisions collaboratively and delegate some of your responsibilities to others by teaching them what they need to know.

> ***Worth Remembering ...*** *"Before you become a leader, success is all about growing yourself. When you become a leader, success is all about growing others." –* ***Jack Welch***

Communicator: If the essence of communication is to send the message and have it received as you intended, then you must keep in mind that you are not the most important person in the conversation. If you cannot communicate in a style that others will understand, then whatever you say will mean absolutely nothing. You must be able to communicate your vision so that others will want to come along.

Decision Maker: Autocratic vs. democratic. Telling people what to do just does not work anymore. If you want others to buy-in to what you are selling, then you need to get them on your side. The only way to accomplish that is to solicit their input and listen to what they have to say. People want to be included, not excluded. Talk it out – find some middle ground that you both can get behind.

Delegator: Resist the urge to micro-manage. Give people the tools they will need to complete the task but stay out of their way and let them do it. Have you ever worked for a micro-manager? Someone who was continually looking over your shoulder, who always seemed to have a better way of doing your job. How did that make you feel? Remember how that made you feel and stop doing it to others.

> ***Worth Remembering ...*** *"Tell me and I forget. Teach me and I remember. Involve me, and I will learn."*
> **– Benjamin Franklin**

If you are looking to enhance your ability to work with others, then learn how to be a better communicator, make collaborative decisions, and resist the urge to micro-manage.

Worth Remembering ...

"The goal of resolving conflict in our relationships should not be about victory or defeat. It should be about reaching an understanding and letting go of the need always to be right."

— Brian Smith

Avoidance is Not Conflict Resolution

*Y*ou cannot ignore a conflict in hopes that it will go away. Avoidance is not the way to resolve conflict. Conflict and disagreements are unavoidable. Whenever you have more than one person in the room, you will have some form of conflict. Two people cannot be expected to agree on everything. When dealt with respectfully and positively, conflict provides an opportunity for both people to grow.

> ***Worth Remembering ...*** *"Creative problem solving is having the ability to directly and positively face and resolve difficult situations." –* ***Unknown***

If you are going to resolve it, you must first understand what caused it. If you do not know what caused it – you are bound to repeat it. Was it competitive feelings, personal jealousy, or resentment? Was it the desire to sabotage someone else's idea, friction caused by poor listening skills, lack of good communication skills or lack of trust? Remember – Avoidance is not conflict resolution. It is not going to go away by walking away. You need to deal with it. No matter how uncomfortable it might be.

Here are five things that you can do to resolve conflict.

1. Provide more information to make discussions more productive rather than contentious. Lack of information or not the right kind of information could be the reason behind the conflict.

2. Ask for solutions. I would never let anyone come to me with a problem without asking them what they would do to resolve it. If their solution sounds reasonable, then do it.

3. Establish common goals. In the big scheme of things, the differences may not be too far apart. You may discover you both want much of the same things.

4. Managing your emotions and keeping your ego in check is key to resolving conflict. Make saving the relationship your number one priority.

5. Do not force a consensus. Come up with a plan that you both can live with. Learn to pick your battles. Sometimes the conflict is not worth damaging or destroying a relationship.

Worth Remembering... *"An eye for an eye will only make the whole world blind." –* **Gandhi**

We are emotional beings, and sometimes we say things in the heat of the conflict that we wish we could take back.

Words are powerful. They can leave an invisible scar that may take a long time to heal. Choose your words wisely.

Second Chances

I hope you got as much out of reading this book as I did in writing it and putting it together. This book is a collection of self-help and personal development articles I've written over the years. I officially turn 70 on November the 9th - 2020. It's nice to be able to check this book off my to-do list before I run out of time.

Experience, good or bad, is a funny thing. It seems the older you get - the wiser you become. The trick is to learn the lessons experience is trying to teach you. Everybody deserves a do-over. Everyone deserves a second chance to do it better the next time.

Worth Remembering ... *"Life gives you a second chance because maybe you weren't ready the first time. Take it!"* **– Unknown**

I hope you're able to learn from my mistakes. God knows I've made a ton of them – and hopefully, I will have the time to make a few more. I say hopefully because that will mean I'm still here. You are never too old to start a new beginning. You are never too old to learn something new.

I dedicated this book to Laura because she has given me a second chance of being in a loving, caring, committed relationship.

I've known her for more than 50 years. Her older brother was my best friend growing up.

He was my best man at my wedding. Facebook made it possible for us to find each other. I am going to make the best of this do-over. I am going to do better this time.

> **Worth Remembering ...** *"If there is even a slight chance at getting something that will make you happy, risk it. Life's too short and happiness is too rare."* **– A.R.Lucas**

Going through a divorce is never easy. Everyone involved pays the price. It put a strain on my relationship with my son.

Chloe, my grandchild, is helping to bring my son and me closer together. I've been given a second chance. I am going to do better this time.

I didn't have a close relationship with my siblings growing up. I don't know if it's because I was a middle child, too old to hang out with my younger siblings and too young to tag along with my older brothers. Family reunions, golf adventures and weddings have brought us closer together. I've been given a second chance. I am going to do better this time.

> **Worth Remembering ...** *"Sometimes things make more sense the second time around. People change, you change and the universe changes. If we keep ourselves confined to first chances only, we will truly miss out on some of the most beautiful things in life."* **– Rania Naim**

Make the best of your second chances. Take the opportunity to start over and do it better the next time.

Acknowledgements

We don't live in a bubble, and we never get anywhere meaningful on our own. We are influenced by the people we meet and the things we see, hear, and read. I have a great many people to thank. They have all impacted my life; all have helped shape me to become the person I am. I have met some of you personally, others I have been influenced by what I have heard you say or by what you have written.

The problem with mentioning people by name is that I may for- get the odd one or two. (You know who you are).

If I have, I hope you will forgive me. Trust me, it was not intentional.

Editing Group:

I'm fortunate to be surrounded by a group of people I trust and whose opinion I respect. A BIG shout out to my proof-reader Laura Handrahan. Your love, feedback, and continued support mean a great deal to me. You make all things possible. A big thank you goes out to Kimb Williams, who helped design the front and back covers. Larry Cavanaugh taught me how to create my QR and ISBN scan code and was instrumental in getting my first book published.

Family & Friends:

A special thank you to the ones who started it all – my Dad Regi- nald Smith, and my Mom – Maggie. I know they are looking down on me – helping to guide my way.

My siblings Greg, Jerry, Terry, Randy, and my sister Laurie. My son Bradley Smith, Emily, my granddaughter Chloe, and Linda. Thank you to my sisters-in-law and all my nieces and nephews, far too many to name them all here without getting into trouble for leaving someone out.

Mentors, Heroes and Supporters at Large

We all need mentors and heroes to look up to – to help inspire and guide us. Someone who leads by example, someone you'd like to emulate. Some of my mentors and heroes I've met, others I've heard speak or have read their speeches or books. They've all impacted my life; they've all had a hand in writing this book in one way or another.

Thank you to the people who I've had the good fortune to work with and learn from. Thank you, Andrew Latendre, Jack Enns, Professor Ron Knowles, Rick Nelles, Drew Mudge, Merv Dillabough, Lionel Conacher Jr., Dave Malcolmson, Clyde Knoll, Greg Johnston, and Wayne McIntyre.

Although we've never met, I've read your books or heard you speak. Thank you, Daniel Pink, Larry Winget, Malcolm

Gladwell, Dale Carnegie, Marcus Buckingham, Maslow, Yung, Covey and Dr. Daniel Goleman.

A big thank you to my favourite speakers, Tom Peters, John Spence, President Clinton, and Obama. It's not enough to think it – and write it – you've got to be able to deliver the material in such a way as to inspire and motivate people to take action.

You have all raised the bar and set the standard that all speakers, presenters, and facilitators should aspire to become.

Index/Notes/References

Introduction

- i

Table of Contents

- Doug Larson – 78
- International Listening Association – 79
- Dr. Ralph Nichols – 79, 80, 82
- Aldous Huxley – 87
- The Shape of Water – 88
- Neil de Grasse Tyson – 88
- Karl Wiggins – 89
- Forest Gump – 90
- Darwin's Theory – 90
- Mark Twain – 91
- Dee Dee Myers – 96
- Anna Crowe – 97
- Huma Gritaz – 97
- Danita Harris – 99
- Thomas Watson Jr. – 102
- Vince Lombardi – 103
- Norman Vincent Peale – 104
- Bud Hadfield – 105
- Sir Winston Churchill – 105
- Amanda Curtis Kane – 105
- Stephen R. Covey – 108
- Viktor Frankl – 108
- Logotherapy – 109
- Napoleon Hill – 109
- Roy T. Bennett – 111
- A. R. Lucas – 113
- Rania Naim - 115

About The Author

Brian Smith – Management Consultant, Published Author and Professional Speaker is an award-winning entrepreneur and former member of the faculty and college professor at Algonquin College's School of Business, having taught Skills for Success, Entrepreneurship and Management Functions 101. With a strong background in working with and leading others as General Manager for a major retailer, Brian understands organizations' challenges today.

Brian specializes in soft-skills training and leadership development. He works with people who want to learn how to communicate and interact more effectively; and who want to discover how to get the best out of themselves and others. Brian is recognized as one of the Top 100 Leadership Experts to follow.

Brian is the author of two previous books - *"Confessions of a Reformed Control Freak – The Top Ten Sins Most Managers Make & How to Avoid Them"* and *"Leadership Lessons from a Reformed Control Freak – The Art of Managing and Leading in the 21 21st Century."*

To find out more about Brian and what he can do for you and your organization, visit his website: https://briansmithpld.com or contact him directly at brian@briansmithpld.com

Confessions of a Reformed Control Freak The Top Ten Sins Most Managers Make & How to Avoid Them

To some extent, the writing of this book was cathartic for me. There's no question that if I knew then, what I know now, I would have managed differently. I hope after reading this book, you will manage and lead others differently as well. "The Top Ten Sins Most Managers Make & How to Avoid Them" are woven into this book's ten chapters. Each chapter is dedicated to one of those sins. And yes – I've committed each one of them at one time or another.

I know from my own experiences what works, and more importantly, what doesn't work. Suppose you want to learn how to communicate and interact more effectively, manage your time, cope with stress, build collaborative teams and better deal with difficult people and challenging situations. In that case, this book is for you. Even seasoned professionals will learn a thing or two by reading this book. Don't put your career or organization at risk. Learn to manage and lead others the 21st Century way.

This book will teach you how.

To order your "autographed" copy, contact Brian directly. Volume discounts are available for large quantity purchases. Email: brian@briansmithpld.com

Paperback online visit Amazon: http://www.amazon.com/dp/1463722273/

E-reader edition for Kindle, Kobo, Apple: http://www.smashwords.com/books/view/125211

Leadership Lessons from a Reformed Control Freak The Art of Managing and Leading in the 21st Century

Whether you are in a management position or play a leadership role in your organization, the challenges remain the same. New skills are required to manage or lead an ever-changing, multi-generational workforce. Success in managing or leading others is no longer dependent on your technical abilities alone. Soft skills, your ability to communicate and interact more effectively with others, now play a more pivotal role in your success. You must master the ability to connect with others to help build collaborative teams, communicate in a way that others will understand, educate them on what they need to know and delegate effectively.

If you want to learn how to build collaborative teams, problem solve, better deal with challenging people and difficult situations or communicate and interact up, down and across the

organization more effectively, then this self-paced workbook is for you. It's filled with exercises, case studies and best practices to reinforce the lessons you'll learn by completing all four modules: Connecting, Communicating, Educating and Delegating.

Additional Bonus

- 24/7 on-going support
- Live Question and Answer Periods
- One-on-One Coaching Sessions for a year
- Certificate upon completion
- Copy of "Confessions of a Reformed Control Freak – The Top Ten Sins Most Managers Make & How to Avoid Them"
- Let's Get Focused Poster
- The Four Step Leadership Development Poster

Let's Get Focused

Enhancing Lives & Transforming Leadership

The Art of Managing and Leading
The Online Course

*I*f you do a Google search for the top ten traits of great leaders, more than likely you will find having the ability to make qual- ity decisions, able to pass work on to others and to be exceptional communicators on that list.

Managing and leading others is a learned behaviour. Are you looking for an online self-paced leadership develop- ment course designed to teach you how to communicate and interact more effectively, motivate others to perform at their personal best, solve problems and build collaborative teams? Then this online course is for you.

Try Before You Buy

Take a test drive to find out if this online course is for you. Take advantage of a **"Free"** lesson on the key to managing and lead- ing others.

Your success is important to me. I want you to take full advantage of all this online course has to offer.

- Unlimited course access
- 24/7 on-going support at no additional cost
- Live Question and Answer Periods
- Your Personal Action Plan for Success
- One-on-One Coaching Sessions for a year

To find out more about this online leadership development course and what it will do for you, follow the link below. Be sure to take advantage of the **"Free"** lesson.

Isn't it about time you got focused?
https://letsgetfocused.teachable.com/p/
learning-to-work-with-others

Let's Get FOCUSED©
A Series of Motivational Speeches and Workshops

rian Smith believes the key to managing and leading in the 21st Century has the ability to connect with others, communicate, educate, and delegate effectively. His *"Let's Get FOCUSED"* © series of motivational speeches and customized presentations is designed to teach you the skills needed to be more successful. Generation.

Brian specializes in **Soft-Skills Training** and **Leadership Development**. He works with people who want to learn how to communicate and interact more effectively; and who wish to discover how to get the best out of themselves and others.

Are you planning an event, seminar or lunch-n-learn? Brian will work with you to create a session that is right for you, your team, and your organization.

Don't put your career or company at risk – learn to manage and lead the ***21ˢᵗ Century Way.***

All presentations can be customized as a 90-minute motivational speech, 2, 4, or 8-hour workshop.

Popular topics in the ***"Let's Get FOCUSED"* © *Series*** of workshops include:

- Managing Others and Living to Tell About It
- Dealing with Challenging Situations Better
- The Top Ten Sins Most Managers Make & How to Avoid Them
- You Don't Have to Like Them – Just Learn to Work With Them
- Powerful Communication Strategies – Bridging The Generational Gap
- Leadership Lessons – The Art of Managing and Leading in the 21ˢᵗ Century
- Who's Got Time for a Nervous Breakdown Anyway? Time Mastery

Additional Bonus: Utilizing group discussion, case studies, and one-on-one consultation, participants will gain the ability to apply what they learn in these workshops. As an added value, we offer on-going support at no additional cost to ensure that participants benefit the most from their participation.

Keep in touch with Brian

Website: https://briansmithpld.com

Email: brian@briansmithpld.com

Phone: 1-613-323-4470

Twitter: https://twitter.com/briansmithpld

Facebook: https://www.facebook.com/
briansmithreformedcontrolfreak/

Linkedin: https://www.linkedin.com/in/briansmithpld/

Instagram: https://www.instagram.com/reformedcontrolfreak/

Youtube: https://youtube.com/user/reformedcontrolfreak

Podcast: https://anchor.fm/brian-smithpld

Made in the USA
Middletown, DE
02 April 2021